THE NEW DUSK

by Richard J Mann

THESCUFFLE.BLOGSPOT.COM
Oliver29jt@gmail.com

1

ABOUT THE BOOK

South Africa's New Dawn rapidly deteriorated into a New Dusk, dense with scandal, violence, corruption, buffoonery in high places and other plagues. The New Dusk is a satirical, sometimes quirky take on this period in the troubled life of our country.

ABOUT THE AUTHOR

Author of Dear Mr Zuma, Dear Mr Malema, Dear Fellow South Africans and South Africa: Stranger Than Fiction. Nothing else is known about him but several psychiatrists are keen to establish contact.

DEDICATION

For Dee

Sincere thanks to many politicians, uncivil servants and public figures for contributing generously to this book.

Dedicated to my large, extended family, with thanks for their support.

Thanks to the encouragers::Lorraine, Allison, Anivesh, Sandy, 'Lady Henry Killinger', Vernon, among others..

CHAPTER ONE

DIS NAG

Literally: 'It's night). Namaqualand expression conveying total incomprehension or utter confusion

June 2021

Pap

I understand how the Pan African Parliament got the name 'pap'.

I listened to a radio broadcast of the proceedings. A cacophony; swearing, yells in several languages - sounds of the average shebeen in full Friday night swing.

'Let me explain how we got here', said the reporter. No need, madam. It is the familiar 'tale told by an idiot, full of sound and fury, signifying', in the elegant phrasing of our own parliamentarians, 'fokol'.

The same happens at the AU, we were told. That's alright then. Comforting. I learnt that the pap is an organ of the AU. If the AU were a person, it would probably be an organ situated somewhere to the rear. Judging by the sounds.

4

The previous chairman, according to our reporter, wanted to continue his influence through his chosen one. 'He wants to rule from the grave.' Mr Malema could probably help him with that.

The uproar seemed to centre on getting a clerk to read a letter. What horrendous challenges the politicians face on this continent. They need our prayers.

Also influencing from the grave were those omnipresent colonialists. We were told that language and colonialism influenced voting. The French speaking bloc sticks together. As does the English speaking bloc. You just can't keep a dead colonialist down.

Throughout the bedlam, a lone voice called out repeatedly: "Call the police."

Hugo, bel die polisie.

June 2021

Bushiri

 Dear Shepherd Bushiri

With today being Sunday, my mind gravitated to matters spiritual.

I'm trying to choose between you and Brother Alph Lukau. Tough choice. Bro Alph has brought at least one person back from the other side. He shattered the myth that you only live once.

You apparently claimed that you can walk on air. Is that how you evaded the South African authorities? South African Airways could have benefited from your expertise. Some cynics maintain that evading the South African police falls far short of the miraculous. I believe you. if I owned four private planes and other expensive goodies, I'd also be walking on air. Just curious as to how you deal with turbulence.

Some say that you are a wolf in shepherd's clothes. Still, there's clear evidence of the miraculous at work. Charges of rape, fraud and other less than sheperdly doings follow you. Yet thousands of followers pour their hard-earned cash into your miraculous enterprises. And hang on to your every syllable. I struggle to gain a hundred followers on Twitter.

In an interview, you blamed racism for negative comments and perceptions. That's a new one.

ECG is an interesting acronym for your church. What would an ecg test reveal about its spiritual heart? No doubt the finances are healthy. You should consider just calling your cul..., sorry, brand of faith 'Bushiri'. It's all about you. Echoes of the Japanese bushido code. You are, after all, a sort of mystic ninja.

Yours in the spiritual struggle.

Richard

June 2021

Giving us a break from the dark, dark political comedy in South Africa, Piet Rampedi broke the news of the birth of decuplets. Then they disappeared off the face of the earth. Mr Rampedi endured much mockery in South Africa and perhaps, even abroad. But here's a logical explanation.

Whatever Happened To Baby Jane...and Baby Joe and...

I am with Piet Rampedi.

The simple truth is that, in South Africa, things disappear. Millions, billions and trillions disappear. Police dockets disappear. An air - walking pastor disappears. A friend's first pension pay-out disappeared. Grown criminals disappear. At the Zondo Commission memory disappears. What is so unusual about ten babies disappearing?

Once more, the deceitful WMC press tries to distract us. Instead of focusing on the real issue, they denigrate Mr Rampedi. The real issue, of course, is:

what is causing the mysterious disappearances? The possibilities are many. I would cast an eye in the general direction of Stellenbosch. A veritable viper's nest of strange and unnatural activities, according to my sources in the RET (no, not that RET; the Relevant Events Trackers) WhatsApp group. Pravin Gordhan, that shadowy manipulator, would be a person of interest too.

Mr Rampedi has been accused of lowering journalistic standards. Not possible. That was done long ago. Just watch certain TV stations and peruse back issues of some newspapers. At any rate, this was as good a story as any I've read in my favourite zombie and tokoloshe hunting publication. A story pregnant with possibilities.

Cynics may ask why the journalist didn't see the babies first. Here's the perfectly reasonable answer, quoted from a news report.

' "In our cultural beliefs, babies and pregnancies are very fragile things. We usually don't like focusing [on] and disclosing such things, especially now that these babies are premature and still in incubators," Mathapelo told local broadcaster Enca at the time, when the news anchor asked her when the world would get to see the babies.'

And now, see what's happened. They were right to be cautious.

June 2021

Pushing Garbage

Are advertisers dumb? Or do they, like many politicians, assume that we are dumb? The garbage from both parties seems to come from the same kitchen.

Still, fun to ponder on if you need an escape from the ANC / EFF / Whats Their Name reality show (the one that makes the Kardashians look like intellectual giants).

If we go by the ads, most of South Africa's problems can be solved by certain brands of bread, booze and over - the - counter pharmaceuticals. Still, I'm willing to give it a shot. I'll bring some loaves to the next EFF or MKMVA march. And some KFC.

'Do you own your skin?', asks one ad. I thought I did, until the question came up. At least on a three score and ten year lease. Is this also covered by Expropriation Without Compensation? Apparently my skin determines how courageous and loving I

11

am. And here I was thinking I might be lacking in moral fibre. It's just a skin problem. Slap on some lotion and bingo! Please send crates to all South African politicians and civil servants.

"Have you ever been turned down for a funeral?" read one on Facebook.

Well, that's a bit difficult to answer. I haven't had need of one - yet. It's going to be harder to answer when I do need one. I don't think it will be my problem anyway.

How about some gritty, relevant ads that reflect our reality.

Here's an example:

Camera lingers on Fred, enjoying a sundowner on his porch, lovingly stroking the shiny, metallic surface of his new acquisition. Voice over:

'Are you afraid that your ten foot electrified fence and pack of Dobermans won't keep you safe? Fear no more. The Gatling 20M will shred everything within a hundred square metres."

"I used to fear the Gauteng sunsets." Fred smiles. "No more."

Fires a practice burst.

"Cheers."

Now that's a realistic advertisement.

June 2021

48 Weeks

In a TV series called The First 48, American detectives set about trying to solve murders, or at least get leads, within a 48 hour window.

It's hard, patient slog. Interviewing potential witnesses, using science and technology, piecing the evidence together, following leads. I admire their persistence, dogged determination and work ethic. No nuclear physics or magic there.

Imagine a similar series in South Africa. 48 Weeks would be a good working title.

Week1

We meet detectives Tom, Dick and Harry hard at work. Picking their way through the pieces, they finally lay bare the bones of the KFC meal.

'My ten years of experience tell me that there's a strong possibility of foul play."

 Sergeant Dick lays out the 200 semi-automatic shells on the table.

"Clearly the shooter or shooters were SANDF - trained."

Detectives Tom and Harry raise quizzical eyebrows.

"200 Shots. Not one hits the target. The man died of a heart attack."

Week 13

We find the detectives working methodically at a Nandos meal.

"Any progress, guys?"

"Yes. Our stolen vehicle's been found. Just the docket missing."

Week 26

"What have we got, guys?"

"A mutton bunny from Gora's."

"No, on the case "

"No-one's come forward to confess yet. Our only witness has moved to Zimbabwe. Harry's out on the decuplet case."

Week 36

Still working doggedly, our detectives have unravelled the mystery of what's at the bottom of the tightly stuffed kotas.

"Good news. We got the ballistics report. It was a semi-automatic. Only a few thousand in the country. The docket turned up in a bin. Just needs some cleaning up. Any luck with the decuplets, Harry?"

Shake of the head.

Week 48

"Don't give up lads. Something will come up. The good news is that I'm off on leave tomorrow. Hang in there. Pass the chips."

June 2021

Fleas

Dear Mr Gigaba

A news report quoted you as follows:

"I knew Mr Ajay and there are many people that we all know, and many get involved in wrongdoing and knowing a person doesn't make you complicit in their wrongdoing if they are involved in wrongdoing."

This strikes a powerful chord with me. An innocent friendship I had was twisted into something ugly. May I share?

I drove some friends to a bank in a powerful, supercharged vehicle. I was delighted to see them comply with health regulations as they pulled on balaclavas and masks. If they had weapons I didn't see them. It was a dangerous neighbourhood anyway.

They returned with bags stuffed with cash. Surely this is normal practice for business people making a withdrawal. I heard of a similar method of carrying cash, used by some powerful people in South Africa. Just can't recall the details.

I did see some of the staff lying on the floor while my friends were inside. I assumed that this was one of those new-fangled business things - power naps or Being Present

As we departed, the police came rushing by, sirens blaring. It was near closing time, but I think the siren thing may be abuse of state equipment.

Ludicrous stories about my involvement in a bank robbery circulated later. Hurtful and bewildering. So easy to be caught in a web of suspicion and speculation. Sir, I empathise.

It is not necessarily true that if one lies down with dogs, one wakes with fleas. Sometimes one wakes with ticks, er, sorry, that's not where I was going. I'm sure you catch my drift anyway.

Yours in the struggle against cynicism.

Richard

June 2021

Vaccines

The EFF marched (what else?) to demand the use of
the Russian and Chinese manufactured Covid vaccines
in South Africa. I support them (what else?), as usual.

Dear Fellow South Africans

It is an established fact that the EFF uses superior
logic. Floyd said so. To the best of my knowledge,
he was sober at the time. I am sure that they
applied their beautiful minds in logical fashion to the
vaccine issue.

I am solidly behind their cause (the same position I
usually take during marches). They must have
mulled over, masticated and digested some of
these indisputable arguments.

1. Who can make vodka like the Russians? I
suspect that the whole cold war thing stemmed
from American envy. Prohibition was nothing but a
cunning plot by those decadent warmongers to
harm the vodka trade. Making vaccines involves
playing around with bacteria or viruses, weakening
them etc.

Making vodka involves playing around with microorganisms in yeast. What's the big deal? In fact, vodka - making is more complex, with the added challenge of finding suitable potatoes.

I could make these things myself (vaccines), with the help of Google, were it not that I've been so busy.

2. I believe that the West has imbued the process with mystery. All the scientific mumbo jumbo is designed to shut out the people. It's the wicked profit motive gone rampant.

3. The Chinese came up with gunpowder, kung fu and acupuncture ages ago. What has the West given us, apart from KFC, medical discoveries, engineering achievements, technological advances and some other stuff? Nothing, I tell you. Democracy, you say. Well, that doesn't work. In South Africa.

Even the vaccine names tell you something. Pfizer sounds like an effervescent solution for digestive problems. Sputnik has an earthy, of - the - people, feet - on - the - ground flavour. I am sure that the Chinese vaccine has a name people can identify with. Something like Heavenly Balm For Eternal, Harmonious Wellbeing.

4. A last, telling point. I have not seen a single sick Russian or Chinese person in South Africa.

Having made the case, I'm happy to take questions on my return from a march.

Yours in the struggle against conspiracies.

Richard

June 2021

South African Cyborg

Dear Mr Musk

The News and Weather channel tells me that you plan to save mankind. I'm all for saving mankind. Your sci-fi like plan to implant chips in the human head had me riveted. I stopped implanting chips in my stomach in order to listen closely. You see artificial intelligence as a potential threat to humankind. In South Africa, it's the lack of intelligence, artificial or otherwise, that threatens us. Particularly in the rarefied atmosphere in which our movers and shakers move and shake.

Nevertheless sir, I have a proposition. I'm willing to be a test pilot, for the sake of humanity, vorsprung durch technik and all those other lekker things. I do this gratis. My only condition is that the chip enable me to beat the lotto and various casino games. This would surely be a worthy test. Also a resounding defeat for one area of AI that's been walloping mankind for far too long. Surely, success will convince even the most sceptical among us.

After a month of lucr.., sorry, intense research and trialling, I would return your chip. What could be more inspirational than having a South African test-drive a brilliant initiative by a South African born innovator? I can see the EFF ground forces marching in support and celebration. I am an excellent candidate, as discretion is my middle - no my first - name. I would keep to myself any winni..., I mean, intellectual property information. Like some South African politicians, I didn't do particularly well at Math Except for algebra, which is surely the most mathematical way of stating the obvious. What else could a + b be but a + b? The point is: if I can crack the jackpot with your technology, what can we / you not achieve? Ready when you are, sir. Yours in the struggle to boldly go where none has gone before. Richard

June 2021 Inspirational Mr Kodwa

An ANC politician tells the Zondo Commission how he managed to get a substantial loan, no strings attached, despite being in an 'unstable' job. There's hope for us.

Dear Mr Kodwa

I was inspired by your presentation. I caught the programme a bit late and assumed that you were giving a motivational talk on tackling tough times. I noticed that several prominent people, including a judge, were listening intently.

What really caught my attention was your account

of snagging a not insignificant loan despite being in an unstable job. Importantly, this was a no-strings-or-elastic-bands-attached arrangement. My faith in the inherent goodness, kindness and generosity of people has been restored. There's hope for me. I have no job, stable or unstable. Still, using your shrewd argument, I believe we can do this. We? I'm hoping that, with your experience and contacts, you can connect me to a philanthropist.

I would also pay once in a stable job. Should that

not happen in my lifetime, it's not a train smash. I'm willing to turn over my assets after departure to destinations eternal. I list them here for transparency: 6 pairs of pants 8 shirts 1 hardly - used suit Assorted underwear and socks 4 potential bestsellers on the Kindle bookshelf. I've sold 8 copies in total but we know that many writers are recognised only after shuffling off the old mortal coil. Who knows what treasure may lie there? Sir, could we meet for lunch (if you could see your way clear to...er. the bill thing..). Yours in the struggle for stability. Richard

July 2021

Realpolitik

Dear Fellow South Africans
Some years ago, I interviewed a young woman who
had started a feeding scheme at her school. The
scheme still feeds over a hundred needy
schoolchildren.
Many of our politicians also started exclusive
feeding schemes. It's not clear how many they
feed. They eat well. The rest of us are, in the words
of Hamlet, promise fed.
King Lear, in the storm, speaking of the 'naked
wretches':

Oh, I have ta'en
Too little care of this! Take physic, pomp
Expose thyself to feel what wretches feel,
That thou mayst shake the superflux to them
And show the heavens more just

But our politicians don't earn enough to have a King
Lear moment. According to some reports. Anyway,
Shakespeare's sentiments are probably un-African.

And all this stuff about compassion and service is too simplistic. The burdens of politics and government are far more complex. It's a silly comparison: a humble, unsophisticated girl feeding over a hundred children. That's not realpolitik.

Yours in the struggle to be realistic.

Richard

July 2021

Relentless

Dear Media People

Dr Ace Magashule was interviewed at inKhaaandla. For some ten minutes he used a lot of words to say absolutely nothing of consequence. It was worse than his famous 'I had a meeting with Zuma but it was not a meeting.....' ramble.
This is clearly a man that has nothing useful or intelligible to say. Why do you foist this nonsense on us? It's not news. 'What we have here is a (massive) failure to communicate' (Cool Hand Luke).
The news anchor congratulated the reporter on his 'relentless' questioning. I missed the relentless part. Where were the questions on why someone who reminds us that he is a leader is not doing what leaders do:

Calming a potentially explosive situation,
Calling for safe, sensible behaviour,
Supporting the rule of law?

As relentless as 'being savaged by a dead sheep' (British politician).

As for Mr Zuma, Mr Niehaus and friends, isn't it

time we gave them a minute each and moved on to really important things. Such as, what we are doing about the relentless disintegration of the foundations of our potentially great country?

After all, the circus one can visit anytime.

Yours in the struggle for real news.

Richard

July 2021
Doctors, Engineers and Teachers Without Borders
Dear South African Recruiters
I am a great fan of South Africa.
I notice that your country has been doing a great job in tackling the unemployment problem. In Cuba and on the African continent. I plan to come over soon. I understand that there's a good flow of traffic at the Limpopo crossing.
I am available for any jobs in healthcare, engineering, math tuition or all of the above. My CV and certified copies of certificates are attached. I did have some misunderstandings with the authorities but have never been cau.., I mean, convicted of a crime. I see that your prominent politicians are strong on the 'innocent until proven guilty' principle. Clearly, the rule of law is paramount.
On that note, I'm very impressed at the leeway given to people to plead their cases. Your former president is my example. He seems a very nice chap. So many friends. I was a little puzzled when I saw only one chap of Caucasian persuasion (looking a little awkward with shield and spear, but still impressive). Given that you are the rainbow

nation. I'm also impressed at how your law seems so open to interpretation and debate. For the people, I suppose. Also, having watched one of your legal people at work (TV news), I think I might even be able to do a bit of that. Weekends maybe. By the way, it's comforting to know that should I ever be charged for a serious offence (e.g. going maskless or accidentally buying alcohol), I have several options.

I look forward to contributing to the great South African melting pot.

Yours in the struggle for a borderless Sou.., sorry, Africa.

Richard

CHAPTER TWO

THE LOOTING CONTINUES

Reaping the ashes

July 2021

Legacy

"Tell us again about the struggle days, Grandpa."

"Well, I'll never forget my first battle. Fists, feet and weapons flying. I fought like a tiger."
"Did you win, Grandpa?"

"I got a TV set and a computer before the police arrived."
"Wow!" The grandchildren look reverently at the large flat screen TV dominating the lounge space.
"After that, you could say I was a veteran. Beer and grocery trucks, factories, schools, you name it. We fought the good fight up and down the province."

"Why did you call it RET?"

"Because we returned the economy to its rightful owners. The people."
"So you took it all back from the oppressors?"

"Yes, we burnt the lot to ashes. Taught them a lesson they'll never forget." "Gosh, Grandpa, you had an exciting life." "Yes, my children." With a grand sweep of his arm, Grandpa takes in the scenery outside. Burnt trucks litter the verges of the roads, blackened skeletons of buildings dot the green countryside. "And one day, all this will be yours."

July 2021

Bravo Mr Cele

Unkind folk said that, in the heat of the crisis, our normally camera-friendly minister of police behaved like a superhero – The Invisible Man

Dear Mr Cele
I must congratulate you on your reassuring appearances on TV and elsewhere during this difficult time.
I apologize for not having actually caught any of them. Been too busy, dodging thugs and looters. I do know, though, that you will have been on top of all this. Just as you were when we were in grave danger from surfers, smokers, boozers and other desperadoes. You handled those in fine style, enabling us to sleep secure in the knowledge that we are protected.
I imagine that you out - sellecked Tom Selleck in Blue Bloods. The calm but steely demeanour. The gravitas. The iconic good guy's black hat. He was only a commissioner and as minister, you have him licked. Besides, he's a Yank and what do they know about real, professional policing. They've never had to hold a desperate, crazed surfer at bay. Or deal with a cunning, law-breaking hawker. Or a

dangerous curfew-breaker. All of which you've done with distinction.

Sir, please let us know when next you will be giving the nation words of comfort and reassurance.
Wouldn't miss it for the world - or what's left of KZN.

Yours in the struggle for law and order.

Richard

July 2021

J' Accuse

Dear Fellow South Africans
"And what dictators do
The elderly rubbish they talk" Auden
Mr Zuma is as pure as the driven snow. Dr Ace
Magashule is Mr Clean on steroids. Julius Malema
and friends are politicians of substance. The ANC is
a movement worthy of respect. Carl Niehaus is a
knight in shining armour, defending virtue and,
especially, truth.
So much for the commercials. Now to some simple
truths.
Mr Zuma and cronies could have prevented this
disaster. But that would have taken real leadership.
And that's rare in South Africa. Real leadership is
selfless. It's for big people.
I cannot say whether Mr Zuma is innocent or guilty
of the many charges hanging over his head. This I
can say: for a man who protests his innocence, the
kindest description of his behaviour is that it's been
extraordinary, bizarre. For one so keen to face his
accusers in a court of law. And the beans he has
threatened to spill? Still on the trellis?

But the ANC is a collective. Let's share blame. Remember the 'pastor' who farts on his congregation. Dear fellow South Africans, if you cannot see how The Party has been doing the same in word and deed for years, stop reading here. Perhaps that's why the poet, e.e cummings wrote that:

'a politician is an arse..'

In our context, that was kind. Even a..ses don't let their houses go up in flames around them. Oh, and it's not on the heads of the ANC only.

If a politician is an a..e, what does that make the placard waving, slogan chanting supporters? There is a simple test for whether a public representative is worthy of your vote. Has he / she built anything of value? Anything lasting. Whether it be tangible or in the hearts and minds of people.

A humble schoolgirl without wealth or authority starts a feeding scheme that feeds over a hundred needy schoolchildren. You follow sleek, well-fed revolutionaries who have never had an original idea. Except to blame, burn and howl curses at the moon. Those who burn seldom build.

Herein lies another simple truth. When the smoke of their abominable sacrifices to the gods of power, greed and hatred dissipates, who will be next?

Such gods are insatiable. They devour their children.
To all you passionate supporters of dubious causes and even more dubious politicians, save that energy. Go build something. Like that schoolgirl.
Yours in the struggle to distinguish between rational thought and brain farts.
Richard

July 2021

Sleep Well Politicians

Dear Shoe - Fitting Politicians
You've had a hard time of it lately.
You have been accused of an entire alphabet of
sins, from asininity, through buffoonery and
corruption to the zumarisation of a once thriving
country.
In Christian charity, I am going to be gentle with
you. I am not going to accuse you of having
handled our current disaster like keystone cops on
nyaope. I will not point out that your intelligence
was as useful as the Titanic's SOS message. Nor
will I compare your troop deployment to locking the
stable door after the entire herd has rampaged
through the neighbourhood. If only you'd done that
with the nimbleness with which large sums were
redeployed on your watch.
I will resist the temptation to comment on your
supernatural powers of invisibility in the heat of
crisis. Followed, of course, by your mystical ability
to materialize at the opportune time.

I vow that I will not snigger at the story of the diligent people's representative. It goes thus. He tells the only people who have stood between their communities and destruction - get this - he tells them to stand down. His version of John vuli gate? (Oh, get behind me satan!). I am sure he will be remembered for this his finest hour, when the sacrifice and the grit of the people of South Africa is spoken of.

May you sleep well.

Richard

July 2021

Bad Dreams

'Oh God, I could be bounded in a nutshell and count myself a king of infinite space, were it not that I have bad dreams.' Hamlet

Dear Mr Malema

Having just woken from a disturbing dream, I feel compelled to write to you.

I saw, in the dream, Floyd The Ferocious, confronting a group of thugs.., sorry, looting gentlemen (slip of political correctness there). He told them to eff off, as this is not the path to economic freedom.

Sir, it got worse. I saw you on a raised platform, craggy features lit by the lights of a dozen raging infernos. You were calling for calm and common sense to prevail. You called on the ground forces to help restore peace and order. Also your air force and navy. The nice thing about dreams is that resources are unlimited.

Then you joined with politicians of all persuasions to discuss ways to end the madness. In the background, were various comrades, soundlessly yelling 'Nooo'. You know the slo-mo, distorted-sound thing in dreams. You turned your back on them and stalked off in true CIC style. It was one of those Stallone / Bruce Willis type scenes. Explosions popping of behind you as you stalked into the sunset.

My own yell was stifled as I sat bolt upright, dripping perspiration onto my newly-changed sheets.

Sir, it was just a dream. Still, as you are often on my mind, I thought it prudent to check. Are you still sound in body, mind and spirit? I trust you've been keeping up with your regular medicals. Please let me know.

Yours in the struggle for economic freedom, land, peace, a united Africa, dialectical materialism and people's banks.

Richard

July 2021

A G.A.T.V.O.L Public Announcement

The Geopolitical Academy for Tracking Viruses Occurring

Locally (GATVOL), makes this announcement in the interests of public safety.

We have identified at least two viruses posing great danger to the health of South Africans.

The Ank virus tricks the body into accepting it as a beneficial nutrient. Once ensconced within the cells, the virus siphons off nutrients until the body is severely malnourished and dehydrated. Interestingly, though subtle at first, the virus grows increasingly voracious with time. Not unlike a herd of swine tucking into a full trough.

This virus often gives rise to several variants. These compete ferociously for dominance, draining the body of any remaining nutrients, energy and strength. They then continue to feed hungrily off the dying body.

The F virus is thought be a variant of the Ank virus. It is similar in some of its behaviour. Also competing with the Ank virus, the F lacks subtlety. It merely rampages through the body. There is no mistaking it for anything but what it is: an entity that exists to wreak havoc and destruction. This variant is thought to be responsible for such conditions as Volatile Behaviour Syndrome (VBS). Under the microscope, it bears a remarkable resemblance to Pacman. Most of its surface resembles a gigantic, wide - gaping mouth. One of our German scientists said that he was reminded of a figure from his country's past history. Pressed for detail, he refused to comment further. "This is science", he said. "Not history ".

Fortunately, the laboratories of

Veracity, Menschlichkeit and Verstand have developed a highly effective regimen. Taken consistently, it rids the body of all variants over time.

South Africans, please be on the alert.

July 2021

What About Kakistan?

I want to distract South Africans from our recent / current troubles. Also to reassure the 'Whatabout' crowd that we are not the only earthlings burning our country about our ears.

The Mann Enterprise for Resolving Dire Emergencies (MERDE) unearthed a fascinating Twitter exchange between government officials in Kakistan. Here's the thread:

@A: Big trouble in Kazedan Province. Burning, rioting, looting. Send army.

@B: LOL. It's not a war.

@A: People will get hurt, maybe die.

@B: People get hurt roller skating. People die choking on fish bones. LMFAO.

@A: This is serious.

@B: So is the locust plague. War is defined as:

a state of armed conflict between different countries or different groups within a country.

SBWL ice cream

A week later

@A: Told you

@B: Still not a war. Anyway we lost only half the province. And a few years. And some smart-alec investors.

@A: This was an insurrection

@B: An insurrection is defined as:

a violent uprising against an authority or government

@A: WTF!

July 2021

The Wisdom Of Jabba The Hutt

Dear TV Producers

A news channel treated us to the wisdom of South African celebrities. Jub Jub's profound insights into the civil unrest were discussed. Whose Solomonic pronouncements will we hear next? Jabba The Hutt?

Some of you may argue that there are people far better qualified to comment. Don't be ridiculous. The man hosts Uyajola, an uplifting programme. He is a hip hop artist. Knows something about racing cars. So what doesn't qualify him?

We've had airtime given to the likes of Dr Ace and the other Zuma Nothing wrong with that. Great content for something other than a news channel. Perhaps our version of America's Funniest Home Videos. We have reporters who remind one of the pain of listening to the kids who wrestled with reading at school. We are fed.

I suggest that the media people take it up a couple of notches. Let's have some drug lords and hijackers share their insights. All in the interests of provoking thought and debate.

My neighbours, Lawrence and Koos are celebrities at Pat's, the local sports bar. With the help of something like Digital Vibes, I can hook you up with them.

Till then, keep up the stimulating stuff.

Yours in the quest for soul-searching, thought-provoking, quality content.

Richard

July 2021

Superior Intelligence

'This week, two ministers gave differing accounts on whether the SSA presented the police with intelligence' - from a news website

Dear Mr Cele

I am concerned about the quality of intelligence that you are receiving. The Mann Enterprise for Resolving Dire Emergencies (MERDE) stands ready to assist. More than I can say for....,sorry, that slipped out.

We have access to unconventional but superior intelligence sources. What's more, they are actually intelligent. Madam Zuzu, our neighbourhood psychic had several visions before the current madness. I did not pay her sufficient attention, as she was halfway through a bottle of gin. She had a vision of livestock being carried through the streets. Also one of a very hungry man watching Masterchef Australia on a brand new big-screen TV. Had I remembered that she accurately and consistently predicted the outcome of most Bafana matches, I would have paid more attention.

We tried to get in touch with a South African celebrity, celebrated for incisive analysis. Unfortunately he was occupied with analysing incidents of cheating on partners. Deep stuff, apparently.

Fortunately, I was able to spend time with our local political commentator, Peter Pompies, over a beer (purchased before the liquor ban). In the measured diction and precise academic language one has come to expect, he said: 'Hier gaan k.k kom''.

Sir, we are ready to share this kind of valuable information with you, going forward. Or backward, depending on how things are handled in your circles.

Yours in the struggle for superior intelligence.

Richard

July 2021

Swine

 We may not be able to defeat these swine, but we don't have to join them.

Bob Dylan

Dear Fellow South Africans

Scrolling through the thought-provoking content on Twitter, I came across a bizarre video clip. I could not identify the country. It couldn't have been South Africa. People were running amok, looting and burning buildings. Things our disciplined cadres would never do.

Here's the bizarre bit. Two men were carrying a live pig through the chaos in the streets. My first thought was: where in the name of Muck did they find a live pig? The second was that it was kind of them to rescue the obviously frightened animal.

I showed a friend. He is a cynic of note.

"Well", said he. "I don't know whether this is a coup attempt or not, but for the pig, that's a fait accompli."

As I don't understand Spanish, I was perplexed.

He went on to say that the practice of carrying pigs was nothing new. In his country, he said, the people bore the burden of sleek, fat (sorry, plus-sized) swine on their shoulders daily. What was new was a couple of swine carrying a third. I was now thoroughly confused.

"Forget about it." I didn't like the glint in his eyes. "They were probably just practicing for the Olympic swine race. We're a cert for gold."

I was as confused as if I'd just heard a classic speech by Dr Ace or a celebrity political commentator.

Please let me have your interpretation, if this makes any sense to you. In English.

Yours in the struggle for clarity.

Richard

July 2021

RET, EFF and History

Dear RET and EFF Gangs

Please note that I use the word 'gangs' with great respect. In its most innocent, innocuous sense. As in, for example, Kool and the Gang. And you certainly embody cool. Tweeting and whatsapping away, not raising a sweat, while the madness rages.

Great strategists are keenly aware of history. Your utterances and recent events tell us that you are firmly in that WhatsApp group. You have clearly studied the Nongqawuse strategem with keen insight. For colonialists, clever blacks and other white - tendencied types who are ignorant of that glorious episode, a summary:

'Nongqawuse claimed that the spirits of the ancestors had spoken to her from a pool in the Gxara River.

If the people would only kill all their cattle and burn their crops, a day would come when new cattle and crops would arise along with an army of the ancestors who would drive the whites into the sea.'

Colonialist history claims that that didn't end well. I would ignore that.

Of course, it would be taking things too far to drive the enemy into the sea. Let the buggers walk. May I ask that you don't use Treasure Beach. The fishing's been good lately.

Much as one hates to reference a white guy, the bile, hatred and blame strategem worked for the guy with the snazzy moustache. Villify in general terms (e.g. 'Juden'). Do it often. Works like a nice, regular dose of arsenic. How's it going for you guys?

Yours in the struggle to reclaim what's left after the cleansing.

Richard

CHAPTER 3

ELECTIONS AND SHENANIGANS

July 2021

Long March

Dear EFF Leadership
I have always been in the vanguard during our historic marches. At least in spirit.
I lost my beret in Brackenfell (not the title of a country song).
I am concerned, though, that the marches are becoming increasingly hazardous. Despite my unquenchable revolutionary fervour, I could not suppress a shiver on hearing that we would march on an old-age home. Do you have any idea how dangerous senior citizens can be? They ran Zimbabwe into the ground. Some say that they are doing the same in South Africa. I was relieved to see community members standing as a buffer between us.
As a committed ground forces member, I obey without thought..., I mean, hesitation. Leaders, do you have any plans for marching on orphanages or homeless shelters? I would like to prepare myself mentally. 'Screw my courage to the sticking place', as some talentless, racist, colonialist, so-called playwright wrote.

I wish to point out that, like our Great Leader, I am willing to kill..,sorry, die for the cause. Living has advantages, though, and I do hope to live to see what's left of the land returned to what's left of The People.

Yours in the long march to freedom and free stuff.

Richard

August 2021

Grave News From G.A.T.V.O.L

The Geopolitical Academy for Tracking Viruses Occurring Locally (G.A.T.V.O.L.) brought you the discovery of the Ank and F viruses in South Africa.

Our motto is 'We dig deeper' and we now bring

grave news. Our research reveals that both variants can cause significant damage in a little-known area of the brain. Scientific name: the conscientia et humanitate lobes. Often called 'skaam cells' by laymen. Indeed, this area may cease functioning altogether with prolonged infection.

The CeH lobes are largely responsible for our

ability to differentiate right from wrong, truth from manure etc. To put it succinctly, this is what restrains the average human being from mugging pensioners.

We advise the public to socially distance from:
Infected public figures,
Deposits of horse manure (interestingly, often found in close proximity to each other)

A complex psychological assessment is used to diagnose and identify. If subjects cannot distinguish between such concepts as 'thuggery', 'protest', 'politics', 'buffoonery' and others, there is cause for concern.

When we asked our scientists about treatment, the most common response was 'Eish'.

However, in other countries, a long (and preferably, permanent) sabbatical has worked wonders.

August 2021

Shuffle On

Dear Fellow South Africans

Being of a sensitive, tolerant disposition, I have some sympathy or empathy for the president.

It's not as if he had a barr.., I mean, bench of the sort the Springboks have. No doubt, he has some duckers and swervers in the Cheslin Kolbe mode. Some, though, don't seem to know which team they're playing for. Some, which game they're playing. Then there are those who couldn't hold on to the ball if their loo.., sorry, lives depended on it.

Haven't we all hung onto stuff that we should have disposed of long ago? Hoping against hope that it might prove useful one day. Tough habit to break. I have a set of ANC, no, AMC Classic cookware that just never gets warm.

I will certainly miss Mr Mboweni. I lived for his lessons on gourmet cooking with garlic and pilchards. He could have taught the comrades a great deal. Mainly that cooking belongs in the kitchen. Cook books and you get burned - or slapped on the wrist.

One thing we all have to agree on: the president had to reshuffle. What with the pack missing an ace.

I'm relieved that our beaches remain safe under the redoubtable Mr Cele. I've been living in fear of ruthless camera crews and surfers. Now it's only the Great Whites one needs to watch out for. But Mr Malema and others have that in hand.

The president knows that track record is important. The best one can say, for now: there seem to be tracks and records aplenty, some of the tracks a trifle muddy.

One does want to be fair (as in impartial, Mr Malema. Not the other..) and give the new ministers space and time. Another 26 years, perhaps?

Hope, it's been said, springs eternal in the human breast. I don't know. I'm still calling Chuck Norris.

Yours in the struggle to shuffle on.

Richard

August 2021
Subtle Rugby Racism

Dear Fellow South Africans
Stop.
Before you have another sip of Castle in celebration of the Springbok victory over the British Lions.
We, in the Movement, are not easily moved by such things. Here's a deep, suitably sombre analysis of what really happened. I am sure that the CIC will issue a succinct, lucid, profound statement in due course. While you wait hungrily for the pearls of wisdom, here's my R200 worth (inflation). I speak as a staunch supporter of dialectical materialism and superior logic.
First, not one player of Indian descent was in the Springbok squad. I did not actually watch the match but I have friends in Phoenix who did.
Second, the black players did all the hard work, as usual. Poor Cheslin Kolbe ran himself into a state of exhaustion. A brilliant try is scored. What happens then? A white guy steps up to put the boot in. The classic apartheid approach.
I could go on about the venue. We have a perfectly good ground in my area. We'd just need to move

some stones. This would have enabled many of my comrades to attend the match. They don't like rugby but it's all about the principle.

I could also talk about the percentage of black players in the Lions squad. I will take that one up with the British embassy at a future march.

Do not be fooled. The racism is exquisitely subtle.

But find it we will.

Yours in the struggle to leave no pebble unturned.

Richard

August 2021

Mr Zuma fell ill before his scheduled court appearance last year. While serving a sentence this year for contempt of court, illness again reared its ugly head. Suspicious and convenient, say some. There's a logical explanation, say I.

Loves To Dance

Dear Fellow South Africans

I would have sprung to the defence of Mr Zuma had I not injured my right calf proving some of the points below. We all know that dancing makes strenuous demands on body and mind. We've seen pictures of the battered feet of ballet dancers. The Mshini dance, though a thing of beauty, punishes the muscles and joints quite severely. Before you nit- picking legal types yell 'calls for speculation', I'll expand. My Defence Of Msholozi (DOM) team and I applied the Mythbusters technique. Testing the dance out on the steps of various courtrooms, we confirmed that the possibility of injury is very real. Mr Zuma may also be suffering from the South African politician's scourge, atypical transient global amnesia, described in great detail in
https://thescuffle.blogspot.com/2020/08/atypical-transient-global-amnesia.html

While ATGA is more a mental / psychological ailment than a physical one, we also know of the mystic linkages between body, mind, soul and other bits.

I hear you say: "What about the suspicious timing?" Oh, the heart of man is inordinately suspicious. Mr Zuma has been looking forward to his day in court for a very long time. The ever-growing excitement as that day approached, must have taken a toll on his battered frame. It could have exacerbated any of the above conditions.

Give the man a break.

Then again, a German lecturer made the profound observation that 'all of life is a break' (Das ganze Leben ist eine Pause).

Yours in the struggle for tolerance and understanding.

Richard

August 2021
Cinders: ANC Fairy Tale

From the province of Dr Ace, philosopher, comes this flash of brilliance.

'The ANC's Free State branch has said that municipalities should intensify their programmes of naming and renaming as a way of speeding up service delivery.'

According to these thinkers, you were wrong, Mr President. There is a magical solution to our troubles. The magic is in the name. Renaming is the fairy godmother who will lift us from the grime of incompetence, indifference, slothfulness and corruption. Into the ball we will sweep, clothed in a shimmering ball gown of service excellence. But we seem to have missed the stroke of midnight and all we are left with are a couple of mice and some thoroughly rotten pumpkins. More correctly, we have swarms of diseased rats.

You need to smoke some incredibly strong, exotic stuff to make such an interstellar leap of logic. Even Durban poison won't do it.

This story has elements of both a zol-induced fairy tale and Orwell's Nineteen Eighty - Four.

Just keep calling incompetence, greed and bull..t something else. In South Africa, we have sufficient numbers of thoroughly dumb or gullible people for this to work better than Orwell ever dreamt.

When reality bites, no problem. We'll find someone to blame it on. Here's a starter list for our Free State comrades. Please add as the spirit moves you:

apartheid, Gordhan, Rupert, Phoenix Indians, DA, WMC and media, counter-revolutionaries, all of the above. I apologize to the many third-force elements and capitalist running dogs that I have omitted.

We'd like to rename your branch but this blog is for family reading.

To quote a little - known Shakespeare line (not William, the other one): 'Manure, by any other name, still smells like s..t'.

August 2021

Crazy Stupid

Have you ever undergone the exquisite torture of desperately needing to laugh at a very inappropriate time?

Happened to me at a meeting at a sister company. I excused myself, found the toilets and - blessed relief - bellowed with laughter. Someone walked out of one of the stalls. I tried to greet him but all I could manage was 'hahaha'. He looked frightened. He also didn't wash his hands.

I had a similar experience listening to the political woes of a friend from Kakistan. It was over a glass of President's Punch at the Saxonworld Shebeen. (Well within curfew and boozing hours, of course). His president reshuffled his lame-duck cabinet. The problem was that the shuffle resembled a before - and - after Taliban photo album. The new speaker had not only duffed up her previous portfolio but now had allegations hanging around her neck to rival the Ancient Mariner's albatross. Adding insult to injury, he said, was her speech about the joys of democracy. He quoted my own favourite Auden verses:

Exiled Thucydides knew
All a speech can say about democracy
And what dictators do
The elderly rubbish they talk

He paused angrily.

"What are you laughing at? It's not funny at all."

"Actually it's a cross between Catch 22 and
Nineteen Eighty -Four". I replied. "Darkly hilarious."
Getting up off the floor: "It's a miracle that you still
have something vaguely resembling a country."
"Barely", he muttered. Then sombrely: "Well you
may laugh. You'll never have to go through that."
"No", I replied. "In our country, we're not that stup..,
I mean, crazy."

August 2021

Bean There, Done That, Mr Zuma

Dear Mr Zuma
I am powerfully moved by your righteous anger and
indignation at 'the law being used to target' you.
I can relate. I was once targeted for doing a mere
thirty kilometres above the arbitrary speed limit.
What kind of law does not bend to accommodate
me..., pardon, I mean emergencies and special
circumstances? For example, the imminent closing
of my local KFC.
Sir, it seems you are on the verge of spilling some
long-promised beans. So moved was I that I had to
borrow from the Langston Hughes poem, with a
minor alteration or two. Apologies to the Hughes
family, friends and poetry lovers.
What happens to beans deferred?
Do they dry up like biltong in the sun?
Or fester like a sore and then run?
Maybe they just sag
Like a heavy load
Or do they explode?

I suspect that we may be at the 'explode' stage. We all know what happens with bean-initiated explosions; the sound, the fury, the stench.

Many South Africans may relate to the original, about a dream deferred. That's not the point. This is about you. After all, which came first: democracy or the ANC?

Sir, I am completely in tune with your implied 'what about others?' argument. During my last court appearance, I pointed out that Al Capone had done far worse. I also once referred my creditors to the national debt, and, for emphasis, the US national debt. To no avail. 'The law is a ass', said one learned gentleman. A soulless ass, some may add.

Sir, let us, like twin Samsons, grasp the pillars and bring the whole edifice down. With our beans.

Yours in the struggle for justice to be done, seen, heard and felt (and smelled?).

Richard

August 2021
Kubi, Mr Mabe

ANC's Mr Pule Mabe on salary payment challenges within the Party, as reported:
"A strange phenomenon has emerged now, especially because we have social media and all of that, when the ANC account and answer to staff, that it is unable to perform because of the challenges it faces. The expectation is that disciplined staff members would then rather ask for a platform with the ANC to understand how the problem is being resolved," said Mabe.

Dear Mr Mabe

Discipline has gone to hell. How dare people go out on social media, complaining about not having been paid?

Would you or I go publicizing family matters on social media? For example, an alcoholic uncle beating the daylights out of family members? No, sir, such sacred family issues must be kept within said family. We must keep a stiff, if somewhat bruised, upper lip. You are the quintessential example. I've not heard you complaining about not being paid.

One sometimes looks back with nostalgia to the disciplined days of strong leaders like Stalin, Kim

Whatsisname and others. I know that decadent pinko liberals will go mad at this; but let's face it, the rack and the thumbscrew had their uses in maintaining discipline in the good old days.

That union bloke, Mr Mdala, reportedly said that management undertook to resolve some of the demands by the end of August. Well, Mr Smart Alec Mdala, it's only the 28th of August.

I think you quite rightly pointed out that this me..,pardon, challenge does not indicate that the Party cannot govern a country. Of course you can. And we'd love to find one somewhere for you to govern. Okay, so we have rampant crime, runaway corruption, incompetence, buffoonery, waste and inefficiency. Apart from that, you guys are doing fine.

Yours in the struggle for discipline.

Richard

August 2021
Angels. Demons and the Mother of

Conspiracies

Dear Fellow South Africans
It troubles me that we are such a divided people.
Scouring social media for wisdom, enlightenment
and other stuff, one stumbles upon chasms of
disagreement and hostility.
Dr Ace, Mr Zuma and other worthies are painted as
angels by one group, demons by another. In the
age of big-brother technology and investigative
journalism, surely we must have evidence one way
or the other.
This puts me in mind of the pro-vaccination / no-
vaccination split. On that note, vaccines may play a
part in the mother-of-conspiracies I am about to
unveil. After the jab, I was overcome by an
unaccustomed surge of hostile feelings towards
both gentlemen. Fortunately, I knew well enough to
chant 'umShini wami' until I entered a trance-like
state of serenity.

To the heart of the matter. Applying the sort of superior logic made famous by the EFF. When people differ so violently against a backdrop of mountains of information, something else is afoot (or in an SUV). MERDE (Mann Establishment for Resolving Dire Emergencies) can now reveal that a fourth force is at play. We face a threat greater than swart gevaar (All Blacks rugby), wit gevaar (Rupert and friends) or any other gevaar. We at MERDE will not be caught napping, unlike the politicians and security clusters of certain countries (not ours, of course). We are on the scent, noses to the ground, stench notwithstanding.

All will be revealed at the same time that the full story of the instigators of insurrection is told. Suffice it to say that a bizarre, sinister plot, involving clones of our saintly heroes has been in operation. It's the clones that solicited and took bribes, frolicked with foreign vegetarians and indulged in other murky adventures. All this, while our heroes wrestled valiantly with cares of state and the welfare of the people (you and me, dear reader). It is thanks to their sterling efforts that we are where we are. Now there's a statement neither camp can disagree with. This mother of conspiracies was partly revealed in Attack Of The Clones
: https://thescuffle.blogspot.com/2020/05/attack-of-clones.html

People laughed then, as they did at Pythagoras, or some other Greek bloke who posited that the earth is round. Until the first ships dropped over the top. Who is behind this? Shadowy organizations and shady individuals. Foreign powers. Think of the riches beneath and above the earth in our country. Coveted by greedy imperialists. Think of the valuable deposits of guano, produced daily by our politicians. Mr Zuma hinted more than once at the dark deeds of legions of spies, domestic and foreign. I was unable to sleep for a week, after his first Zondo Commission appearance. In the fullness of time, MERDE will reveal all. Till then, yours in the struggle against fourth force conspirators. Richard

September 2021

Mr Zuma refused to have state – appointed doctors examine him. I understand.

I, too, avoid physicians, Mr Zuma

Dear Mr Zuma

While employed by a primary health care clinic, I fell ill at work.

"You need to see a doctor", advised a colleague. I went off and was back ten minutes later. My colleague was surprised.

"Did you see the doctor?"

"Two of them", I replied. "Walking down the corridor. I feel better now."

Sir, I tell this story to illustrate that I share your wariness (perhaps suspicion) about doctors. I have discovered the following about them:

1. They have no boundaries and ask the most embarrassingly intimate questions about bodily functions. "Do you have regular bowel movements?" For Pete's sake!

2. They have a very negative attitude. Every time I've been to one, he or she has found something wrong. It's never "Wow, your blood is circulating so well - and in the right direction too", or "Gee, that stomach is almost perfectly round." Words of comfort and inspiration in these difficult times when our favourite political parties are falling apart.

3. They lie. "I'm going to shove this metre long needle into your arm and you'll feel better in no time."

4. They give bad advice. "Lay off the wine, women, song and good, red meat and your quality of life will improve."

I ask myself how different they are from the shamans who peer into chicken entrails but can't give a simple lotto combination.

We are, if not in the same boat, at least on the same marina.

Yours in the struggle against poking, pummelling physicians.

Richard

September 2021

When the ANC appeared to be imploding under the weight of scandals, acts of corruption and internal battles.
Long Live

Dear ANC

That looked like a rather sudden, swift slide to mini-implosion. Truth is, though, it was inevitable. You should have seen it coming. You cannot dig holes and rip pieces off the slide without interesting consequences. Vision and foresight haven't been your strong suit. Hard to see the wood when you're preoccupied with the size, colour and location of each tree. I do think reports of your demise are premature. You have history on your side. And food parcels, grants, clichés, song and dance. I'm sure that, like a character in a certain type of movie, you will rise again to haunt..., I mean, to fight on. Yeats wrote of a once beautiful, young woman: I know not what the younger dreams - Some vague Utopia - and she seems, When withered old and skeleton - gaunt, An image of such politics

Politics of the stomach and the empty cliché can also do that. Only balloons rise on hot air.

And Yeats might have had you in mind with:

Why, what could she have done, being what she is? Was there another Troy for her to burn?

Yours in the struggle to adapt.

Richard

September 2021

Exodus

Dear Fellow South Africans

Elections approach. Time to look back in anger or wonder or bemusement or amusement. Or all of the above.

In the Book of Exodus, Moses parted the Red Sea with his staff. In the case of the ANC, the staff were often sleeping, goofing off or off on weird and wonderful adventures. The tender for a Red Sea freeway left us stranded, wet and bedraggled.

Moving on, here's a quick guide to the parties vying for your suddenly precious vote.

The DA will fight for your rights once they have finished fighting among themselves. With a good reputation for governance, they lack the theatre arts to reach a nation fed on Durban Gen, Uyajola and the bovine cud that passes for TV news.

The ANC are big on culture. Storytelling, dance (including the popular 'Step Aside'), comedy and drama are but some of their offerings. Fiction is the preferred genre. They sometimes wander off into the horror realm. Also good at the fine arts, they've become renowned for drawing lines in the sand.

The EFF will march at the drop of a beret. Possessed of a substantial ground force, they will be hard to resist once they acquire a navy and air force. To those who see the EFF as noisy populists, not ready to govern, think again. They have interesting views on banking and can be called very business savvy or VBS - for short. Add to that, great dress sense and an appreciation of the finer things and you have a force to be reckoned with. In the fashion world. COPE were not available for comment. For all that the Freedom Front Plus have achieved an FF- would probably be a fair score. Let's not forget the new parties and the smaller parties, unless they lose their way (as often happens) on this gruelling exodus. Then, by all means, forget them. Yours in the struggle to reach the oft-promised land. Richard

September 2021

Downhill Racers

Dear ANC

It's not fun to make fun of you anymore. I was brought up right.

It's like mocking a drunk who's fallen into a pit latrine. I'm going to have to stick to the EFF. Incidentally, an irate ground forces member wanted to know if I entertain myself with fantasies. No, I replied, the EFF entertains me - royally. The fantasies I leave to them.

At any rate, it's really hard to keep up with your disasters and scandals. Like watching an overcooked disaster movie. You know: monsters, aliens, floods, fires, and quakes, all in one gigantic, unappetizing stew. Or like playing one of those alien invaders games. The more alien ships you shoot down, the faster they keep coming. And they never stop.

Could you perhaps do a roster of scandals, failures, looting achievements, blunders, embarrassing moments, nonsensical utterances and the other stuff you excel at? Like the Eskom loadshedding thing. You could call it the Bullshedding Thing. That way, we could keep track. Feel free to use the categories above as headings. You could put the task out to tender.

George W Bush once said something along the lines of: "Our enemies will do everything they can to destroy our country. So will we" An unfortunate choice of words. For you, though, a perfectly lucid statement.

You out-stooge the Three Stooges at their ridiculous best. You gave us Hlaudi, Mr Zuma, Dr Ace, Eskonomics, Flying Without Wings at SAA, tenderpreneurs, ANCspeak and so many other gifts that keep on giving.

It's hard to make fun of you. You do it so well yourselves.

Yours in the struggle to remember what we're struggling for.

Richard

September 2021
Edward's Grapes of Wrath

Dear Mr Edward Zuma

There have been times that the whole world has
trembled at the prospect of imminent disaster. I
believe that such a time is again upon us.
Our neighbourhood has started a prayer chain, as
people did during the Cuban missile crisis. You
have warned us that the whole world will see your
anger. I am sure that it is a fearsome thing.
I have friends who laughed at your reaction, on TV
news, to the Concourt ruling on your respected
father's rescission application. I warned them that
you are a serious man. After all, like a popular
politician, you were willing to die for the cause. After
padlocking the gates of the inKandla homestead.
I tried to make sense of your ranti.., sorry,
discourse. I cannot capture the eloquence of your
address but garnered the following gems:
Not only is the judiciary captured and bought, but
also full of pride. That's a couple of deadly sins right
there, sir.
Said judiciary made a nonsensical ruling.
Compounding this are the reporters with their

nonsensical reporting. (I have indeed heard and seen some nonsensical stuff on TV news - unrelated to your matter).

You will not do or encourage anything illegal. Then again, you don't 'recognize any legality' in this country. You see my slight bewilderment here, sir?

You will march daily in protest until the judiciary admit their mistake. Sackcloth and ashes, surely, as they repent having been 'eaten by pride'. I suppose that shouldn't take too long.

Otherwise you will react very badly. Does this include swearing and slamming doors? Disturbing stuff, sir.

When you mentioned people in red, sitting on benches and bringing the country into disrepute, I thought you were taking a swipe at EFF MPs.

You almost called Mr Manyi 'Jimmy'. A miniscule slip in a speech reminiscent of the best of Churchill (not Winston, my neighbour, Zeke Churchill).

Sir, by your (and your esteemed father's) report, your family appears to be much sinned against. Judges, spies, reporters, ministers, sinister others - all hurling fiery darts. It's a wicked world.

Yours in the struggle for justice and reason.

Richard

September 2021
Mampara of the Century

Dear ANC

I watched the news on my neighbour's new, big-screen TV today. He acquired it sometime in July, during the disturbances. Driven by pangs of hunger, he was cruising the Durban streets in his SUV, when he saw the TV set lying outside a Game store. Assuming it to be surplus stock, he thoughtfully gave it a good home.

With today being Heritage Day, we wore our traditional masks, had a traditional KFC meal and viewed the traditional offerings by the national broadcaster. Edward Zuma accused the media of nonsensical reporting. I don't know. The recorded news broadcast was as up-to-the-minute as usual. If there had been interviews, I am sure that they would have been as incisive as usual. Cutting through the politicians' newspeak to the buried truth.

We watched South African Airways staff and supporters dancing as the national carrier took to the skies again. Caught up in the moment and giddy with joy, we also danced the Jerusalema and the Step Aside. And bellowed out a rousing rendition of 'Flying Without Wings'. For the poor, this is a meaningful investment. We can stand shoulder to shoulder (not literally - social distancing applies) with politicians queuing for their free flights to Cape Town. There will surely also be jobs aplenty: pilots, aircraft mechanics, steal..., I mean, sorting luggage. A Union Person shared the wisdom that it would be bad for workers if the ANC were to be, (mercy on us all!), defeated at the upcoming polls. In other news, it was reported that the ANC has not paid or cannot pay their workers for some time. I was mildly confused. Some unkind souls suggested that you should be the Sunday Times' collective Mampara of the Year. That's grossly unfair. You deserve Mampara of the Century. Yours in the struggle against mamparadom. Richard

September 2021
I thought that, in our brave new country, censorship was no more.

Censored
A social media contact from Iran told me that he was having trouble accessing my blog. Later he messaged again to say that he'd found out why. Iran, he said, was blocking and censoring. I responded with the calm demeanour that maturity brings. After I'd thrown out the Persian rugs in a rage and torn up my air ticket to Tehran. One learns to rise above pettiness. On the same day, a South African online magazine followed suit. They had invited me to submit articles but about four articles down the track, this was forwarded to me: "The satire articles we are getting from ***** seems to be getting some negative comments... This may eventually cause a stir in the political arena... I am of the view that put a moratorium on it to protect the publication sector"

Such interesting bedwet..., sorry, bedfellows.

Good people, the whole point and purpose is to
cause a stir in the 'political arena'. That does read
suspiciously like: "We really don't want to upset
some people." That kind of cow.., pardon, cautious
approach is not unusual. Unnecessary, perhaps, as
it's unlikely that the ones we fear offending actually
read. Apart from the classics and the government
gazette.
Interesting bedfellows indeed.

September 2021

Slow Learners

"Tune in for a saga of lies, scandals and corruption", urged the TV voice.
I dutifully tuned into the news. It was an advertisement for a soapie, instead. Well, they're going to have to up their game to compete with South African news broadcasts.
I vaguely recall ANC claims that 85% of households have been electrified. Questions about the sources of statistics aside, I suppose it's an achievement over 27 years. What I do know is that the ANC has kept 100% of households electrified with their shenanigans. Comedy, family feuds, pillaging, crime, bizarre utterances and more, kept us transfixed.
Clichés and acronyms have flown thick and fast - RET, WMC, BBEE, BEE, Integrity, revolutionary, our people decent jobs etc. Fortunately, most have proven to be meaningless, so please don't weary yourself deciphering them.

By the by, perhaps I'm being cranky, but can we not set up a presidential press briefing where one can actually hear the questions being asked? It's in the little things, said Aristotle.

The president reassured us that the ANC is now learning from a past they are not proud of. I've heard of slow learners, but 27 years.... Still, Mr President, I'm sure that your party will muddle through. It's possible that there are some slow learners among the voters, too.

In other news, a city official bemoaned the poor work of housing contractors in a residential area. "If a contractor builds shoddy houses", he said. "He should not be given another opportunity".

Ja, well, I don't know.

October 2021

Saving the zebra

 I learned from TV news that Covid is responsible
for an increase in teenage pregnancies. That's at
odds with what my biology teachers taught, but who
am I to argue?
Political promises dominated the rest of the news,
so my mind drifted inexplicably to fables and fairy
tales. Here's one I heard in southern Africa.
In a green, pleasant land lived various animals,
ruled by the vultures. Why vultures? It's a fable.
The cruel, selfish vultures took most of the land for
themselves and made absurd laws, restricting the
movement of all other animals. This was particularly
hard on the zebras, who loved to run free. They
became weak, sickly and dispirited.
A band of noble hyenas overthrew the vultures, to
the delight of all the other animals. Noble hyenas?
Its a fable, for Pete's sake. Besides, if you're South
African, that's not the most bizarre thing you've
heard today. Hlophe and Mkhwebane have been
nominated for the Chief Justice role.
The hyenas introduced regular leadership elections
and promised many good things. The champagne
taste of freedom was in the air.

However, as often happens in fables, a shaft of gloom penetrated the light. The hyenas secretly sold large tracts of land to humans, who slashed and burned. Some of them fed off the older zebra and the young. The animals were outraged.

At election time, the hyenas were contrite. They would deal with all rogue hyenas through several hyena committees. Had they not fulfilled some promises? Would they not fulfill many more? Some animals were placated. One of the hyenas could not resist nipping at the calf of a zebra.

The party of the red-breasted squawkers loudly proclaimed that this was nonsense. They held the keys to the land of free things. To the zebras they said: "Your white stripes are the cause of all your troubles. We will rid you of them."

And, for emphasis, they marched around, hurling insults and curses at the white stripes.

Then all the animals chimed in, until the very hills reverberated with baying, howling, barking and hooting

But some of the animals quietly wondered:

"Who will save the zebras?"

October 2021

Phoenix

 Dear ANC

Thank goodness for the DA's propensity for shooting themselves in both feet.

What a grand opportunity for a flamboyant display of unrighteous indignation. You can cover a multitude of sins with this gift of the gods of political opportunism. And boy, we are talking a multitude. To list them would turn this post into a facsimile of War and Peace. You do know that we're talking of the Phoenix election posters. I can barely bring myself to type the name without breaking out in hives.

Interestingly, a commentator pointed out that the president and others praised people for defending their communities. But that's beside the point. Whatever said point may be.

You ought to use this opportunity like the mythical phoenix. Revive it from the sad ashes of your own sorry campaign at every opportunity. Why not raise a monument? We could have a danger - tape cutting ceremony. But let's go frugal; no more than a million.

Mr Cele spoke a while back. It was with a passion that we've not seen when he discourses on all the boring violence and murder elsewhere in the land. The timbre of his voice swelled with gravitas as he uttered the magic word: 'racism'. It was like seeing an otherwise placid person transformed by a stiff dose of speed.

A suitably grave TV person spoke of 'playing with people's lives'. I thought that's what we'd been witnessing for many decades. Is that not the whole political game in our country?

Pious and sanctimonious sentiments descended like the Durban rain. I was reminded of Auden's:

In the nightmare of the dark

All the dogs of Europe bark

(Substitute anything for Europe).

Two things come to mind. One: just the matter of perspective. Two: why is made to sound as if the Phoenix community is entirely made up of mass murderers?

Yours in the struggle for perspective.

Richard

October 2021 Blah Wars: The Search For The Jedi

The Ancites can make things disappear with a wave of the hand. Or flourish of a pen. I thought that I had at last found the mystical brotherhood of the Jedi. But all was not well. The dark side was strong within them. Rumour was that many had gone over. Planet Zuma, Planet Ace and many of the stars that had once made up the Republic now seemed to lie in darkness and confusion. I sought out the rebel leader, General Seeyisee, With his strong convictions and vast army of clones, the general may have held hope for the Republic. But, as Yoda would have put it: 'Strong the force could be in him, but darkness there is. Contradictions too many, there are. Flip-flopping and the anger strong. Afraid I am that he is vulnerable to the temptations of the dark side.' The blue army of the Defiance Alliance wielded their light sabres with great skill at times. Then, at others, they tripped over their own feet. Falling down and falling out often just as they seemed about to rise to the occasion.

Throughout the Republic, many other parties lay claim to the Jedi heritage. Many are untested or have discovered the power of invisibility, sometimes spoken of in hushed tones among believers.
The search for the Jedi continues.

October 2021

Going To The Dogs

Dear SIU, Hawks and Other Crime busters
People say that South Africa is going to the dogs.
While self-respecting dogs may bridle at that
suggestion, it did spark off an idea. May I, in all
modesty, add, a brilliant idea.
We've long known that dogs can sniff out
explosives, drugs and accelerants. Now, more
excitingly, there are indications that they can also
sniff out various illnesses and diseases.
What is the greatest threat to the stability and
progress of our beloved country? Corruption, of
course. It's been described as an epidemic.
Applying the superior logic gained from observing
EFF leadership, corruption can therefore be
categorised as an illness.
I suggest that we begin training corruption-sniffing
dogs forthwith. While dogs sniff armpits for disease,
I imagine that our canines would focus on the
stomach area. One would expect a richer, riper
scent than that emanating from other ailments.

With an eye to our EFF comrades on the ground, I suggest that we don't use the popular European breeds. The use of German Shepherds, Belgian Malinois and English Springer Spaniels could lead to accusations of racism and neo-colonialism. Bruno is a Wentworth, Durban - born dog of uncertain, but indisputably South African origin. He already shows great promise, having seen off several election campaigners in fine style. I see him as a pioneer in this new war on corruption. A sort of first among equals. I'm working on the tender proposal, with other local dog owners and trainers. We will be needing a veritable army of trained canines. Just a hunch. Yours in the out-of-the-box approach to the grim struggle against corruption. Richard

October 2021 A World In One Country

Like the president, I am shocked. Indeed, shell-shocked. My analyst, Dr von Schollenhofen von Eltern unter den Tannenbàumen, diagnosed PTSASD (post- traumatic South African stress disorder). Curable only by nine holes of golf. It's been a week from hell. Taking politicians hostage is bad enough. Stupid, of course. Who, in their right minds, would pay a ransom for a South African politician? But to attack a Shisa Nyama owner! Cold-blooded brutality. That's the last bastion of service delivery in South Africa. Elsewhere, scenes reminiscent of Blackhawk Down, as alleged Somali traders burn taxis. Mr Cele was on the scene in what seemed like seconds. The US, the UK and other less-developed nations (than ours) tend to have the local chief constable, police chief or commissioner respond in such situations. We send in the big hats..., I mean, big guns. That's why we are so far advanced. In all sorts of things. I was present and saw a group of dubious-looking fellows with firearm bulges in various places. They were shaking with what could have been mistaken for laughter. I knew that it was fear. It's working, Mr Cele. It can only get better. It can only...

We are streets ahead of the US. They have the mafia (which doesn't really exist) and various crime corporations. In South Africa, you can hire a disposable hitman at Black Friday rates all year round.

Makes one proud to be South African.

To those hysterical alarmists who interpret the recent avalanche of disasters as meaning that the barbarians are at the gates, I say: "Don't be ridiculous." The gates are firmly locked.

The barbarians are safely within.

October 2021 For What Does It Profit...

Call me naive (I prefer 'innocent'). I hear persistent, ridiculous rumours of our country having been sold for a plate of vegetarian curry. That's absurd. No meat! For a mutton curry, one might momentarily consider trading a very small piece of unused municipal land. There has to be a logical explanation. Here's my best shot. The gentleman in question was reportedly made a pastor by some men of the cloth. Moved, no doubt, by, if not the spirit, then some spirits. In the enthusiasm of the moment, he may have read of Esau's giving up of his birthright to Jacob, in exchange for a meal. It's possible that he merely got the direction of the transaction slightly wrong. A perfectly understandable slip twixt cup and lip. Such trade-offs are nothing new in South Africa. For all the talk of socialism and dialectical materialism, hated capitalism and the despicable profit motive are alive and well. Indeed, fat and flourishing. We are a world leader in futures trading. Even now, while election promises fly like great flocks of Kimberly flamingos, some continue undeterred to trade our future for gourmet meals. Or sushi and tripe.

Our politicians are deeply concerned for the poor. I imagine that it hurts each time they chew on another morsel of the fat of the land. I bet it irks to have bodyguards, free travel, expensive accommodation and other irritants thrust upon them. They're probably muttering in their restless sleep: "That money could have gone to development" It's tough up there. No, more accurately: it's agony.

In the courtroom scene of A Man For All Seasons, a former friend betrays Thomas Moore for advancement to Attorney General of Wales.

"For Wales? Why Richard, it profit a man nothing to give his soul for the whole world ... but for Wales!"

October 2021

Smoke Gets In Your Eyes

Music to get you into the election mood:
They asked me how I knew
My party was true
Oh-oh-oh-oh,

 I, of course, replied
"The pledge that they have signed
Cannot be denied"
 (Ooh, ooh, ooh)

They said, "Someday you'll find
Loyalty is blind"
Oh-oh-oh-oh
When the braai's on fire
You don't realize
Smoke gets in your eyes
I ignored them
As I made my mark
To think they would doubt our crowd
Yet today, my bunch has gone astray
The ink has hardly dried
Now, laughing friends deride
Tears I try to hide
Oh-oh-oh-oh

So, I smile and say "As
the braai flame dies
Smoke gets in your eyes"
Smoke gets in your eyes
Smoke gets in your eyes
Smoke gets in your eyes

October 2021

A Lighter Shade Of Grey

Jolly election song, to the tune of A Whiter Shade
Of Pale

They dance a fierce fandango

Turn cartwheels around the facts
I am getting kinda seasick
But the crowd yells out for more
It is getting so much harder
And sanity just flew away
Then I thought I'd have another drink
But someone stole the tray

And so it was that later

As the politician told his tale
That my face, at first just cloudy
Turned a lighter shade of grey

They said, 'Listen to reason'

But the truth is plain to see
So I wandered through the history
And could not let it be
Some three hundred and more parties
Will be vying for my vote
And although our eyes are open
They might just as well be closed

And so it was that later
As the campaigner told his tale
That my face, at first just cloudy
Turned a lighter shade of grey

www.ingramcontent.com/pod-product-compliance
Lightning Source LLC
Chambersburg PA
CBHW051259020426
42333CB00026B/3274